WINDOW ZIPS

ZIPPERED VINYL POCKETS IN MEMORY PILLOWS

Memories are visible when tucked inside a pocket pillow. Clear
vinyl windows on the appliqued pocket allow all to share the joy
within. Each pillow becomes an individual expression as it is filled
with important momentoes.

BY MARILYN ROBINSON

TABLE OF CONTENTS

Photography - Brian Birlauf
Illustrations and Graphics - Marilyn Robinson, Sharon Holmes, Lynn Pike
Editor - Sharon Holmes
© 1992 Marilyn Robinson
Published in the United States of America by *Possibilities®,* Denver, Colorado 80231.
ISBN:0-9622477-9-0
First Printing 1992

STAR PRIZES

SUPPLIES:

Fabric (44″ or 112 cm wide, shrinkage allowed):
  Front and back - ⅝ yd. (.6 m)
  Upper star - 8″ x 12″ scrap
  Lower star - 10″ x 18″ scrap
  Outer ruffle - 1⅛ yd. (1.1 m)
  Inner ruffle - 1 yd. (1 m)

Optional:
  Fabric markers or dimensional fabric paints

Other:
  9″ sport zipper (23 cm)
  14″ nylon zipper (36 cm)
  Paper-backed fusing web - ½ yd. (.5 m)
  Stitching stabilizer - ½ yd. (.5 m)
  Clear vinyl (8-gauge) - ⅓ yd. (.3 m)
  Thread to match applique fabrics

DIRECTIONS:

1. Cut one 17″ square for pillow front. Cut one 6″ x 17″ rectangle and one 12½″ x 17″ rectangle for pillow back.

2. Follow step 1 only of MACHINE APPLIQUE, page 18, to cut out *upper star* and *lower star*. (If applique fabric is lighter than background, see NOTE at end of machine applique directions.)

3. Insert sport zipper between *upper star* and *lower star*. Paper backing is still in place. See SPORT ZIPPER, page 18.

4. Following step 2 of MACHINE APPLIQUE, peel paper backing off paper-backed fusing web (such as Wonder-Under™). Position star on 17″ square front according to layout on next page. Press *upper star* first, flattening seam along zipper. Flip vinyl to *upper star*; smooth *lower star* and press, being very careful not to touch iron to vinyl.

5. Straight stitch vinyl close to edge of *lower star*. An even-feed foot is great for this, or lay tissue paper on top of the vinyl if it wants to stick to presser foot. Trim vinyl to meet edge of *lower star*. Trim ends of zipper to meet applique edge.

6. Follow steps 3 through 5 of MACHINE APPLIQUE, page 19. Stitch all the way around star. Pivot on curves and be sure to catch ends of zipper in satin stitch. Unzip 2″ to 3″ when approaching left side of zipper for a flatter stitching surface.

7. Put zipper in pillow back. See BACK ZIPPER, page 18.

8. Trim corners of pillow top and back. See TRIMMING, page 19.

9. Add ruffles. Pillow shown on cover has a double ruffle. Cut 4 strips 9″ x 44″ for outer ruffle and 4 strips 7″ x 44″ for inner ruffle. Sew 4 narrow strips together end to end; sew 4 wider strips together end to end. Trim longer ruffle to same length as shorter ruffle. Sew ends of inner ruffle together to form a loop; sew ends of outer ruffle together to form a loop. Fold each ruffle in half lengthwise and press. Lay inner ruffle on top of outer ruffle, raw edges together. Stitch ruffles together with ¼″ seam. Proceed with step 3 of RUFFLES, page 20.

10. Finish. See FINISHING and PILLOW FORMS, page 20.

11. Optional: Use fabric markers or dimensional fabric paints for signatures around star.

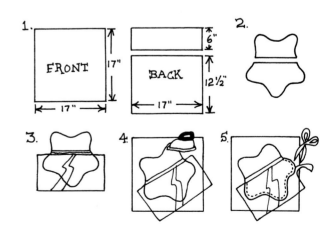

PUT IT IN YOUR POCKET

Wrapped candies
Friends' photos
Ticket stubs
Fancy erasers
Pencils
Key chains
Baseball cards
Award ribbons
Scout badges
Jewelry
Friends' autographs on background
Special letters
Trip momentoes
Party invitations
Photos from school events
Words to favorite song

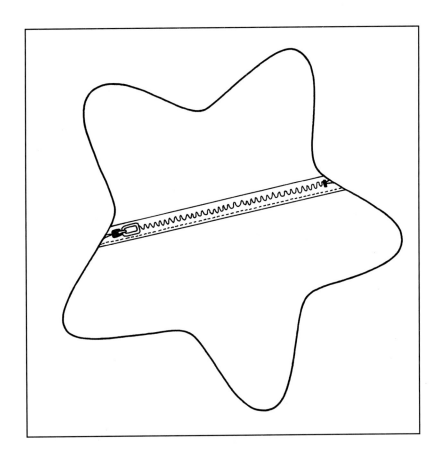

A SPECIAL PLACE TO SHOW OFF SUCCESSES AND SURPRISES. YOUR CHOICE OF FABRICS WILL MAKE IT APPROPRIATE FOR CHILD OR TEEN, BOY OR GIRL.

BIRTHDAY   SCHOOL PLAY   SPORTS AWARD

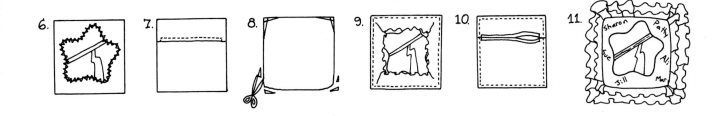

HELLO BABY

SUPPLIES:

Fabric (44″ or 112 cm wide, shrinkage allowed):
    Front and back - ⅝ yd. (.6 cm)
    Cloud - ⅓ yd. (.3 cm)
    Baby body - 4″ x 6″ scrap
    Baby head - 3″ x 3″ scrap
    Stars - 3 scraps 5″ x 5″
    Cording - ⅓ yd. (.3 cm)
    Ruffle - ⅞ yd. (.8 cm)

Other:
    7″ flat cotton lace
    9″ sport zipper (23 cm)
    14″ nylon zipper (36 cm)
    Paper-backed fusing web - ¾ yd. (.7 cm)
    Stitching stabilizer - ½ yd. (.5 cm)
    Clear vinyl (8-gauge) - ⅓ yd. (.3 cm)
    Thread to match applique fabrics
    Cording (#80) - 2 yds. (1.9 cm)

DIRECTIONS:

1. Cut one 17″ square for pillow front. Cut one 6″ x 17″ rectangle and one 12½″ x 17″ rectangle for pillow back.

2. Follow step 1 only of MACHINE APPLIQUE, page 18, to cut out *baby head, baby body, upper cloud, lower cloud,* and *stars*. (If applique fabric is lighter than background, see NOTE at end of machine applique directions.) Leave paper backing on *upper cloud* and *lower cloud*. Peel backing off *baby body* and place in position on cloud according to layout on next page. Press. Peel paper backing off *baby head* and place in position. If creating a baby boy, go ahead and press. The girl requires lace slipped just under edge of head before pressing. Zig-zag lines indicated on pattern for eyes.

3. Insert sport zipper between *upper cloud* and *lower cloud*. Paper backing is still in place. See SPORT ZIPPER, page 18.

4. Following step 2 of MACHINE APPLIQUE, peel paper backing off paper-backed fusing web such as Wonder-Under™. Position cloud on 17″ square front according to layout on next page. Slip *stars* into position under edge of cloud. Press *upper cloud* and upper *stars* first; flatten seam along zipper. Flip vinyl to *upper cloud;* smooth *lower cloud* and press, being very careful not to touch iron to vinyl. Press lower *star*.

5. Straight stitch vinyl close to edge of *lower cloud*. An even-feed foot is great for this, or lay tissue paper on top of vinyl if it wants to stick to presser foot. Trim vinyl to meet edge of *lower cloud*. Trim ends of zipper to meet applique edge.

6. Follow steps 3 through 5 of MACHINE APPLIQUE, page 19. Stitch around *stars* first, then around *baby head* and *baby body*. Begin at upper left *star* on cloud and stitch all the way around cloud. Pivot on curves and be sure to catch ends of zipper in satin stitch. Unzip 2″ to 3″ when approaching left side of zipper for a flatter stitching surface.

7. Put zipper in pillow back. See BACK ZIPPER, page 18.

8. Trim corners of pillow top and back. See TRIMMING, page 19.

9. Add cording. See CORDING, page 19.

10. Add ruffle. Pillow shown has a 3″ finished ruffle. Cut 4 strips 7″ x 44″. See RUFFLES, page 20.

11. Finish. See FINISHING and PILLOW FORMS, page 20.

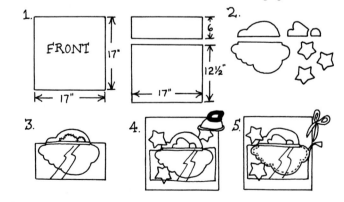

PUT IT IN YOUR POCKET

Baby photos
Bracelet, ring, or locket
Bubble gum cigar
Lock of hair
Birth announcement
Small cards
Dried flower from bouquet
Footprint on paper
First haircut photo
Newspaper headline from birthdate
List of favorite toys
Baby spoon
Diaper pin
Baby booties
Baby shower invitation
Small cap

FOR THE SWEET REMEMBRANCES OF THOSE FLEETING YEARS. A WONDERFUL
PRESENTATION TO A NEW BABY OR TO SAVOUR THE JOYS OF ONE GROWING UP.

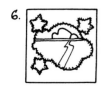
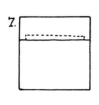
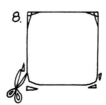

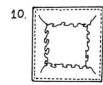
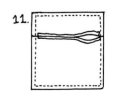

HEARTS AT HOME

SUPPLIES:

Fabric (44″ or 112 cm wide, shrinkage allowed):
Front and back - ⅝ yd. (.6 m)
Upper house - ¼ yd. (.3 m)
Lower house - ¼ yd. (.3 m)
Chimney - 2″ x 3″ scrap
Hearts - 3 scraps 3″ x 3″
Cording - ⅓ yd. (.3 m)
Ruffle - ⅞ yd. (.8 m)

Other:
9″ sport zipper (23 cm)
14″ nylon zipper (36 cm)
Paper-backed fusing web - ½ yd. (.5 m)
Stitching stabilizer - ½ yd. (.5 m)
Clear vinyl (8-gauge) - ¼ yd. (.3 m)
Thread to match applique fabrics
Cording (#80) - 2 yds. (1.9 m)

DIRECTIONS:

1. Cut one 17″ square for pillow front. Cut one 6″ x 17″ rectangle and one 12½″ x 17″ rectangle for pillow back.

2. Follow step 1 only of MACHINE APPLIQUE, page 18, to cut out *chimney*, 3 *hearts*, *upper house*, and *lower house*. (If applique fabric is lighter than background, see NOTE at end of machine applique directions.)

3. Insert sport zipper between *upper house* and *lower house*. Paper backing is still in place. See SPORT ZIPPER, page 18.

4. Following step 2 of MACHINE APPLIQUE, peel paper backing off paper-backed fusing web (such as Wonder-Under™) on all applique pieces. Position house on 17″ square front according to layout on next page. Place *chimney* in position under edge of roof. Press *upper house* and *chimney* first; flatten seam along zipper. Flip vinyl to *upper house*; smooth *lower house* and press, being very careful not to touch iron to vinyl. Flip vinyl down. Place *hearts* in position. Press.

5. Straight stitch vinyl close to edge of *lower house*. An even-feed foot is great for this, or lay tissue paper on top of the vinyl if it wants to stick to the presser foot. Trim vinyl to meet edge of *lower house*. Trim ends of zipper to meet applique edge.

6. Follow steps 3 through 5 of MACHINE APPLIQUE, page 19. Stitch around *chimney* first. Next, stitch around 3 sides of *lower house*. Pivot on curves and be sure to catch ends of zipper in satin stitch. Unzip 2″ to 3″ when approaching left side of zipper for a flatter stitching surface. Stitch around all sides of *upper house*, including along zipper seam. Finish applique by stitching around the 3 *hearts*.

7. Put zipper in pillow back. See BACK ZIPPER, page 18.

8. Trim corners of pillow top and back. See TRIMMING, page 19.

9. Add cording. See CORDING, page 19.

10. Add ruffle. Pillow shown has a 3″ finished rufffle. Cut 4 strips 7″ x 44″. See RUFFLES, page 20.

11. Finish. See FINISHING and PILLOW FORMS, page 20.

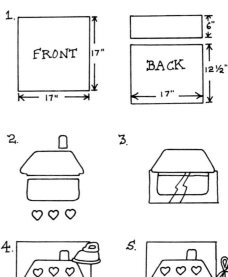

PUT IT IN YOUR POCKET

House key
Dried flower from the yard
Seed packets
Moving announcement card
Photos of neighbors
Photos of the house/garden
Recipes from the neighbors
Tea Bag
Family photo
Moving day photos
Address label
Postcard of new home state
Business card
Child's drawing of house
Real estate card
Small cross stitch

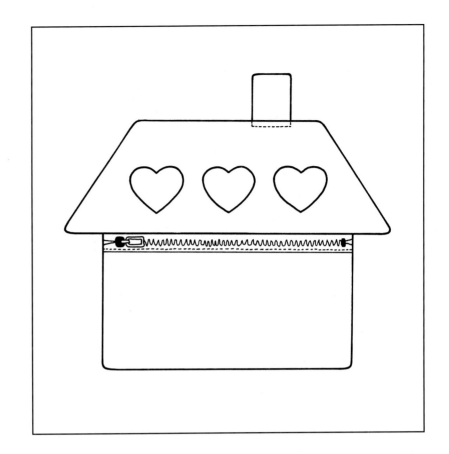

ONE ALWAYS LEAVES A PART OF ONE'S HEART BEHIND. THIS PILLOW TAKES ALONG PRECIOUS MEMORIES TO THE NEW HOME OR WELCOMES A NEW FRIEND TO THE NEIGHBORHOOD.

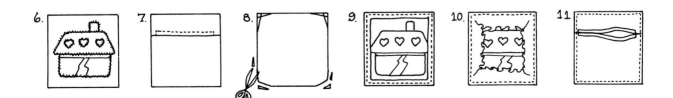

TRAVEL TREASURES

SUPPLIES:

Fabric (44″ or 112 cm wide, shrinkage allowed):
    Front and back - ⅝ yd. (.6 m)
    Postcard - ⅓ yd. (.3 m)
    Cording - ⅓ yd. (.3 m)

Optional:
    Fabric markers

Other:
    9″ sport zipper (23 cm)
    14″ nylon zipper (36 cm)
    Paper-backed fusing web - ½ yd. (.5 m)
    Stitching stabilizer - ½ yd. (.5 m)
    Clear vinyl (8-gauge) - ⅓ yd. (.3 m)
    Thread to match applique fabrics
    Cording (#80) - 2 yds. (1.9 m)
    Dimensional fabric paint

DIRECTIONS:

1. Cut one 17″ square for pillow front. Cut one 6″ x 17″ rectangle and one 12½″ x 17″ rectangle for pillow back.
2. Follow step 1 only of MACHINE APPLIQUE, page 18, to cut out *upper card* (address side) and *lower card* (pocket side). (If applique fabric is lighter than background, see NOTE at end of machine applique directions.)
3. Insert sport zipper between *upper card* and *lower card*. Paper backing is still in place. See SPORT ZIPPER, page 18.
4. Following step 2 MACHINE APPLIQUE, peel paper backing off paper-backed fusing web (such as Wonder-Under™). Position card on 17″ square front according to layout on next page. Press *upper card* first, flattening seam along zipper. Flip vinyl to *upper card*; smooth *lower card* and press, being very careful not to touch iron to vinyl.
5. Straight stitch vinyl close to edge of *lower card*. An even-feed foot is great for this, or lay tissue paper on top of vinyl if it wants to stick to presser foot. Trim vinyl to meet edge of *lower card*. Trim ends of zipper to meet applique edge.
6. Follow steps 3 through 5 of MACHINE APPLIQUE, page 19. Stitch all the way around card. Pivot on curves and be sure to catch ends of zipper in satin stitch. Unzip 2″ to 3″ when approaching left side of zipper for a flatter stitching surface.
7. Put zipper in pillow back. See BACK ZIPPER, page 18.
8. Trim corners of pillow top and back. See TRIMMING, page 19.
9. Add cording. See CORDING, page 19.
10. Finish. See FINISHING and PILLOW FORMS, page 20.
11. Add stamp, name, and address with dimensional fabric paint. Optional: Use fabric markers to reproduce postmark.

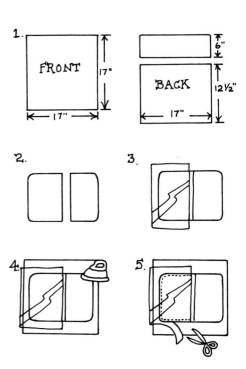

PUT IT IN YOUR POCKET

Postcards
Souvenirs
Key chain
Sea shells
Sand
Photos of those visited
Candies
Brochures
Business cards
Match covers
Photos of people visited
Airline ticket
Special event ticket
Napkins from restaurants
Section of a map
List of places visited
Festive confetti

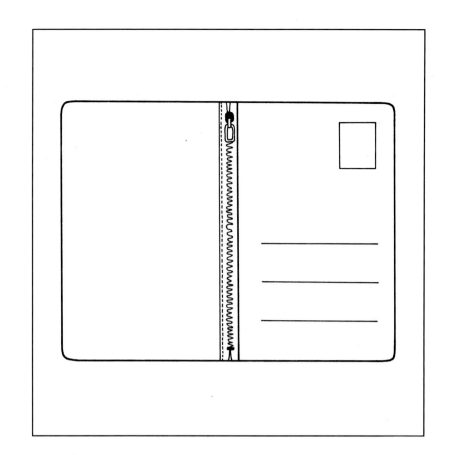

WHAT A WONDERFUL TRIP! THE PHOTOS AND SOUVENIRS COLLECTED ON THAT VENTURE WILL ALWAYS RECALL THE FUN EXPERIENCED.

VACATION

REUNION

DESIGN A STAMP!

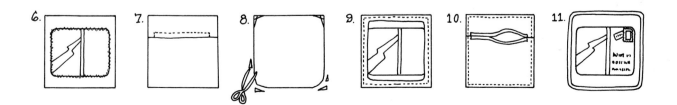

PAST PIECES

SUPPLIES:

Fabric (44″ or 112 cm wide, shrinkage allowed):
  Front and back - ⅝ yd. (.6 m)
  Upper triangle - 9″ x 9″ scrap
  Lower triangle - 9″ x 9″ scrap
  Star points - ⅛ yd. (.2 m)
  Outer ruffle - 1 yd. (1 m)
  Inner ruffle - ⅓ yd. (.3 m)

Other:
  9″ sport zipper (23 cm)
  14″ nylon zipper (36 cm)
  Paper-backed fusing web - ½ yd. (.5 m)
  Stitching stabilizer - ½ yd. (.5 m)
  Clear vinyl (8-gauge) - ¼ yd. (.3 m)
  Thread to match applique fabrics

DIRECTIONS:

1. Cut one 17″ square for pillow front. Cut one 6″ x 17″ rectangle and one 12½″ x 17″ rectangle for pillow back.

2. Follow step 1 only of MACHINE APPLIQUE, page 18, to cut out *upper triangle, lower triangle,* and *8 star points.* (If applique fabric is lighter than background, see NOTE at end of machine applique directions.)

3. Insert sport zipper between *upper triangle* and *lower triangle.* Paper backing is still in place. See SPORT ZIPPER, page 18.

4. Following step 2 of MACHINE APPLIQUE, peel paper backing off paper-backed fusing web (such as Wonder-Under™) on all applique pieces. Position square star center on 17″ square front according to layout on next page. Place eight *star points* in position ¼″ under edges of square star center. Press *upper triangle* and *star points* first; flatten seam along zipper. Flip vinyl to *upper triangle* and smooth *lower triangle.* Adjust lower star points if necessary. Press, being very careful not to touch iron to vinyl.

5. Straight stitch vinyl close to edge of *lower triangle.* An even-feed foot is great for this, or lay tissue paper on top of vinyl if it wants to stick to presser foot. Trim vinyl to meet edge of *lower triangle.* Trim ends of zipper to meet applique edge.

6. Follow steps 3 through 5 of MACHINE APPLIQUE, page 19. Stitch around *star points* first. Pivot on curves. Next, stitch all the way around square, catching ends of zipper in statin stitch. Unzip 2″ to 3″ when approaching left side of zipper for a flatter stitching surface.

7. Put zipper in pillow back. See BACK ZIPPER, page 18.

8. Trim corners of pillow top and back. See TRIMMING, page 19.

9. Add ruffle. Pillow shown has a two-toned, 4″ finished ruffle. Cut 4 strips 2″ x 44″ for inner ruffle. Cut 4 strips 7½″ x 44″ for outer ruffle. Sew 4 narrow strips together end to end; sew 4 wider strips together end to end. Sew long edges of the 2 strips together with a ¼″ seam and press before constructing ruffle. See RUFFLES, page 20.

10. Finish. See FINISHING and PILLOW FORMS, page 20.

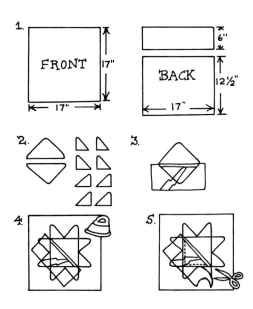

PUT IT IN YOUR POCKET

Doily
Small piece of patchwork
Small scissors
Thimble
Tape measure
Ribbon
Photo of loved one
Business cards from favorite shops
Cross stitch
Small pattern
Paper doll
Scrap of lace
Antique photos
Package of needles
Seam ripper
Decorative beeswax

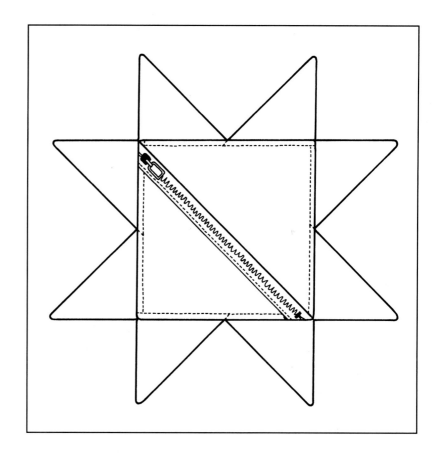

EVERYONE CAN BE A STAR FOR A DAY. REMEMBER TALENTS AND TREASURES OF THOSE IN YOUR LIFE WITH A BEAUTIFUL TRIBUTE.

AWARD   BIRTHDAY   THANK YOU

EDUCATED PLACES

SUPPLIES:

Fabric (44″ or 112 cm wide, shrinkage allowed):
 Front and back - ⅝ yd. (.6 m)
 Upper school - ⅓ yd. (.3 m)
 Lower school - ¼ yd. (.3 m)
 Cording - ⅓ yd. (.3 m)

Optional:
 Dimensional fabric paint
 ½″ jingle bell

Other:
 9″ sport zipper (23 cm)
 14″ nylon zipper (36 cm)
 Paper-backed fusing web - ½ yd. (.5 m)
 Stitching stabilizer - ½ yd. (.5 m)
 Clear vinyl (8-gauge) - ¼ yd. (.3 m)
 Thread to match applique fabrics
 Cording (#80) - 2 yds. (1.9 m)
 ½″ ribbon - ½ yd. (.5 m)

DIRECTIONS:

1. Cut one 17″ square for pillow front. Cut one 6″ x 17″ rectangle and one 12½″ x 17″ rectangle for pillow back.
2. Follow step 1 only of MACHINE APPLIQUE, page 18, to cut out *upper school* and *lower school*. (If applique fabric is lighter than background, see NOTE at end of machine applique directions.)
3. Insert sport zipper between *upper school* and *lower school*. Paper backing is still in place. See SPORT ZIPPER, page 18.
4. Following step 2 of MACHINE APPLIQUE, peel paper backing off paper-backed fusing web (such as Wonder-Under™) on *upper school* and *lower school*. Position school on 17″ square front according to layout on page 17. Press *upper school* first, flattening seam along zipper. Flip vinyl to *upper school*, smooth *lower school* and press, being very careful not to touch iron to vinyl.
5. Straight stitch vinyl close to edge of *lower school*. An even-feed foot is great for this, or lay tissue paper on top of the vinyl if it wants to stick to the presser foot. Trim vinyl to meet edge of *lower school*. Trim ends of zipper to meet applique edge.
6. Follow steps 3 through 5 of MACHINE APPLIQUE, page 19. Stitch around 3 sides of *lower school*. Pivot on curves and be sure to catch ends of zipper in satin stitch. Unzip 2″ to 3″ when approaching left side of zipper for a flatter stitching surface. Stitch around all sides of *upper school*, including along zipper seam.

7. Put zipper in pillow back. See BACK ZIPPER, page 18.
8. Trim corners of pillow top and back. See TRIMMING, page 19.
9. Add cording. See CORDING, page 19.
10. Finish. See FINISHING and PILLOW FORMS, page 20.
11. Tie bow with ½″ ribbon and stitch or hot glue to bell tower. Optional: Stitch or hot glue jingle bell under bow; add child's name and school year with dimensional fabric paint.

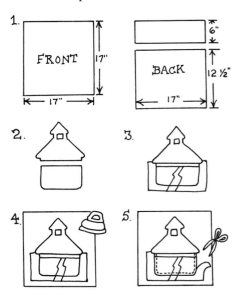

Continued on page 17

STAR PRIZES, page 2

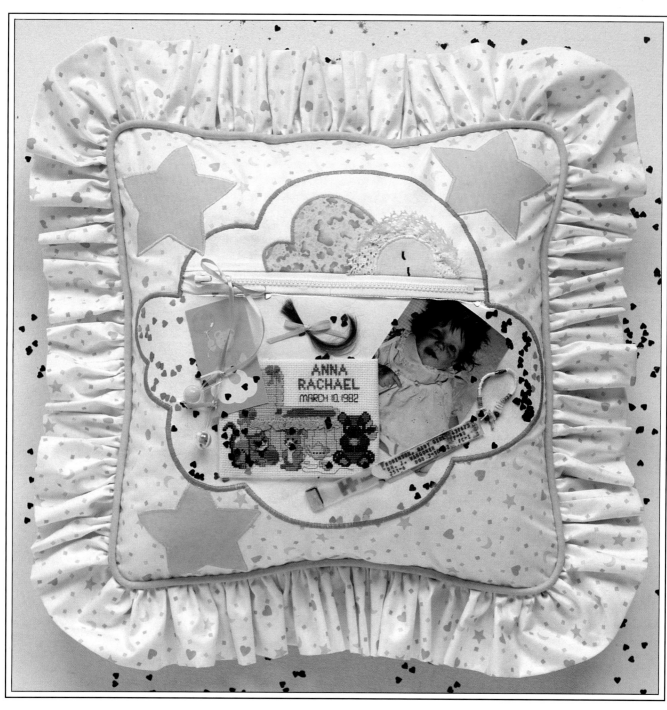

HELLO BABY, page 4

HEARTS AT HOME, page 6

EDUCATED PLACES, page 12

TRAVEL TREASURES, page 8

PUT IT IN YOUR POCKET

Library card
Student I.D. card
Award ribbons
Photos of school friends
Calculator
Buttons
Programs from special events
Pencils
Erasers
Child's drawings
Copy of report card
Notes from a teacher
Special certificates
Section of music page
Lunch ticket
Old school papers

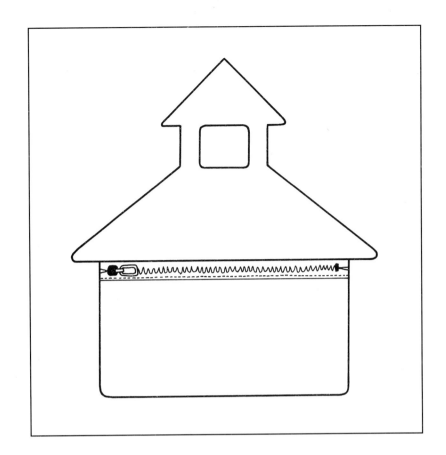

GOOD OL' GOLDEN RULE DAYS ARE LONG REMEMBERED BY KEEPSAKES TUCKED INSIDE THE SCHOOLHOUSE. A CLEVER WAY TO TRACK THE YEARS!

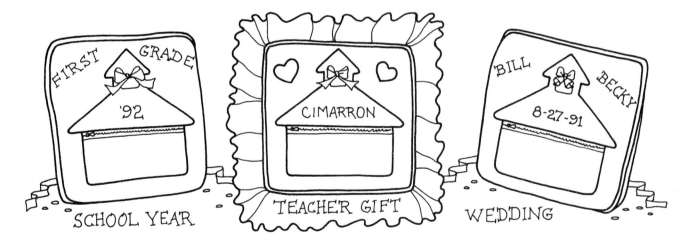

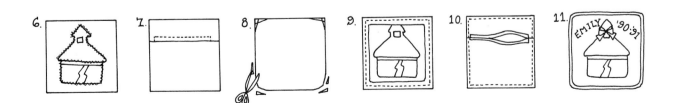

TECHNIQUES

PUTTING IN THE ZIPPER

SPORT ZIPPER (FRONT OF PILLOW)

1. Each applique has an upper and lower section. Lay lower section right side up. Place closed zipper right side up, long edges together, tab at left, and raw edges of fabric even with top edge of zipper tape. Make sure ends of zipper reach ends of applique. Pin center and ends. Unzip 3″.

2. Lay upper section right side down on top of zipper. Pin.

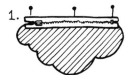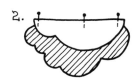

3. Using zipper foot, stitch ³⁄₁₆″ from raw edge. Stitch the first 2½″, leave needle down, lift presser foot, and close zipper. Continue the seam the length of the zipper. Open and finger press seam toward upper section.

4. Cut vinyl 1″ larger on all sides than lower applique piece. Use ruler and cut a straight edge along top side.

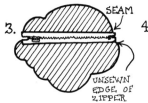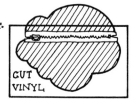

5. Lay cut edge of vinyl along bottom edge of zipper tape and stitch ³⁄₁₆″ from edge. Placing a narrow piece of tissue paper on top of vinyl will help zipper foot along. Thin tissue paper will allow you to still see the seam allowance.

6. Flip vinyl over to expose zipper teeth. Distance between seams should measure ¾″. Adjust seam depth if necessary. Fold seam (both vinyl and zipper tape) toward zipper teeth and topstitch zipper tape close to fold, catching the vinyl underneath. Tissue is not needed. Reposition lower section under vinyl. The vinyl piece should amply cover the lower applique.

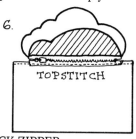

BACK ZIPPER

1. To make a lapped zipper, begin by laying the 6″ piece of backing on top of the 12½″ piece, right sides together and raw edges even. Sew a ¾″ seam for 1⅜″. Lengthen the stitch to basting and stitch 14¼″. Return stitch to regular length and finish seam. Press seam open. Reposition to expose one side of seam allowance.

2. Open zipper and place one side face down on extended seam allowance with teeth on seamline. Machine baste ¼″ from zipper teeth.

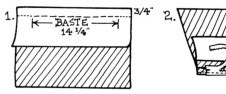

3. Close zipper and turn zipper right side up, leaving all fabric to one side. Stitch along narrow fold next to zipper teeth.

4. Spread fabric flat, right side up; pin zipper and then stitch along ends and top of zipper ½″ from seam. Remove basting. Back should measure 17″ x 17″.

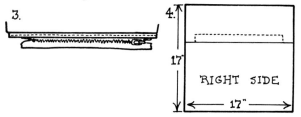

MACHINE APPLIQUE

Any fabrics may be used, but my personal favorite is 100% dressweight cotton. It presses beautifully and won't ravel. If all fabrics in the pillow contain the same fiber content, they won't require special handling. Good quality cotton thread gives a smooth, satin finish and is available in a wide selection of colors.

1. Trace pattern onto paper side of paper-backed fusing web (such as Wonder-Under™), reversing the image. Cut out at least 1″ outside of drawn line. Press adhesive side of paper-backed fusing web to back of applique fabric. Cut out applique shape on the drawn line.

2. Peel paper from applique and position on background, overlapping pieces when necessary. Iron into place.
3. Place stitching stabilizer (such as "Stitch-n-Tear"®), under pillow front. Use a very short stitch length and approximately ⅛" wide zig-zag stitch. Narrower zig-zagging may be used on applique pieces not containing the zipper, but a minimum of ⅛" is necessary to catch the zipper securely. It helps to practice this stitch on a scrap first.
4. Keep threads of satin stitch at right angles to edge of applique by pivoting on curves. To pivot, leave needle in fabric, lift presser foot, rotate fabric, lower foot, and resume stitching. Pivot with needle in background fabric for outside curves. Pivot with needle in applique fabric for inside curves. On tapered points, reduce stitch width when approaching point; increase it again when going away from point. To tie off threads, bring stitch width to zero and take 5 to 6 stitches next to satin stitching. Trim threads.

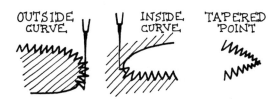

5. Tear off background stabilizer when finished with all applique.

NOTE: If background fabric shows through applique fabric, applique piece may be backed with white muslin. Before cutting out applique shape, layer fabric, fusing agent (such as Stitch Witchery), and white muslin. Press. Bond paper-backed fusing web to white muslin side of layered fabric. Trace patterns onto paper side of fusing web and cut out. Most light fabrics overlaying a darker background will need to be backed.

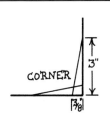
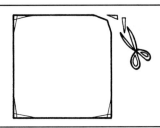

TRIMMING

1. Lay front and back of pillow right sides together.
2. Mark corner trimming lines as shown.
3. Using sharp scissors, cut on drawn lines. This step will eliminate sharply pointed corners on finished pillow.

CORDING

1. To make bias for cording, draw lines on fabric at a 45° angle to the selvage, 1¾" apart. Draw and cut enough strips to equal 72" in length when sewn end to end.
2. Sew strips end to end with ¼" seams. Press seams open.

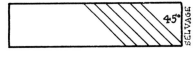
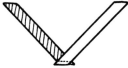

3. With wrong sides together and strip folded lengthwise, lay 2-yard piece of cording inside folded strip. Using a zipper foot, machine stitch next to cording, but not too close.

4. Pin cording to right side of pillow front, raw edges even (½" seam allowed). As you turn corners, clip to stitching on cording. Start stitching on side of pillow, 1" from one end of cording. Stop stitching 1½" from end. Cut off cording, allowing 1" to overlap.

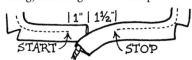

5. Pull back casing and clip cord so that ends of cording will meet when fabric is pulled back over them.

6. Fold casing under about ½" and stitch remainder of cording to pillow edge. Nice, smooth finish!

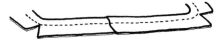

RUFFLES

1. Two widths of ruffles, 3″ and 4″, have been used on the pillows in this book. Determine the finished width you desire, double this measurement, and add 1″ for the seam allowance. The length of the ruffle strip is approximately 2¼ times the distance around the pillow. This makes it easy to simply cut four strips the width of the fabric (44″). The desired ruffle width determines how wide you cut the strips. Cut strips 9″ wide for a 4″ ruffle and 7″ wide for a 3″ ruffle. Trim off selvages.

2. Sew short ends of ruffle strips together using ¼″ seams. Make a complete loop. Press seams open. Fold in half lengthwise, raw edges even, and press. Fold loop into four equal sections and mark each fold with a pin.

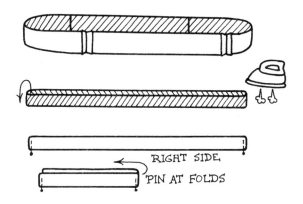

RIGHT SIDE
PIN AT FOLDS

3. Measure 2 lengths of thread, enough to go around edges of pillow. Knot them together at one end. Using a narrow zig-zag, anchor knot ⅜″ from raw edges of folded ruffle. Use a wide zig-zag and hold threads in one hand. Pull gently as the machine zig-zags over the threads, gathering as you stitch. Zig-zag around entire loop taking care not to catch threads in zig-zag stitch.

3/8"

4. Pin gathered ruffle to right side of pillow front, raw edges even, matching pins to corners. Gather ruffle to fit. If laying ruffle over cording, make sure cording is kept away from stitching line. Stitch ½″ from edge, smoothing fullness of ruffle as you go. Make sure corner has plenty of gathers to allow for spreading when pillow is turned.

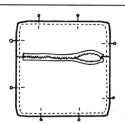

FINISHING

1. Partially unzip back of pillow. Lay face down on top of pillow front. Pin along edges.
2. Stitch together, taking caution to sew just inside previous stitching so that none of it will show when pillow is turned.
3. Turn pillow right side out.

PILLOW FORMS

1. Purchased pillow forms are fine, but for a smoother pillow, try making your own. Cut two 18″ squares of fleece or needlepunch.
2. Lay pieces together and stitch around outside edge with ½″ seam, leaving an opening for turning.
3. Turn right side out and put in fiberfill which has been fluffed and spread apart with your fingers. Don't overfill.
4. Stitch the opening closed.
5. Insert form into back of pillow, adjusting into corners. The 17″ pillow form inserted into the 16″ pillow makes the pillow cover fit smoother.

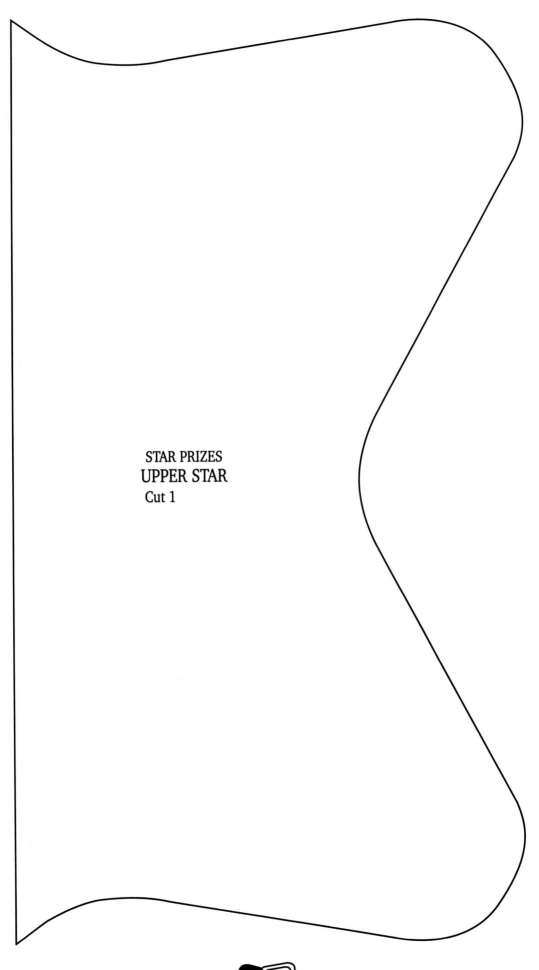

STAR PRIZES
UPPER STAR
Cut 1

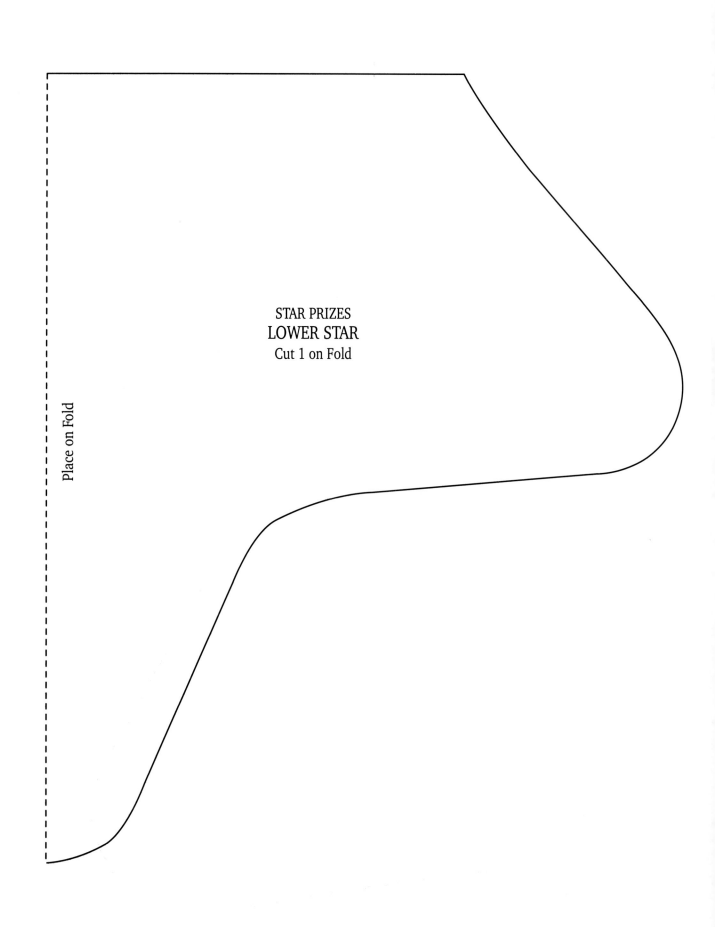

STAR PRIZES
LOWER STAR
Cut 1 on Fold

Place on Fold

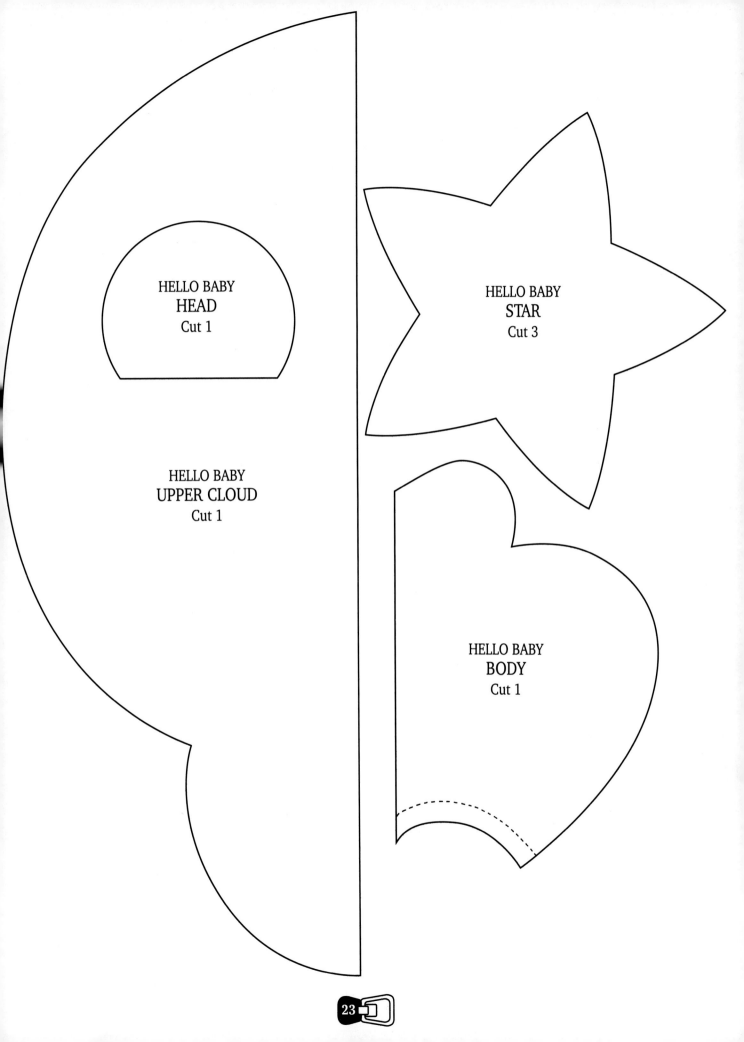

HELLO BABY
HEAD
Cut 1

HELLO BABY
STAR
Cut 3

HELLO BABY
UPPER CLOUD
Cut 1

HELLO BABY
BODY
Cut 1

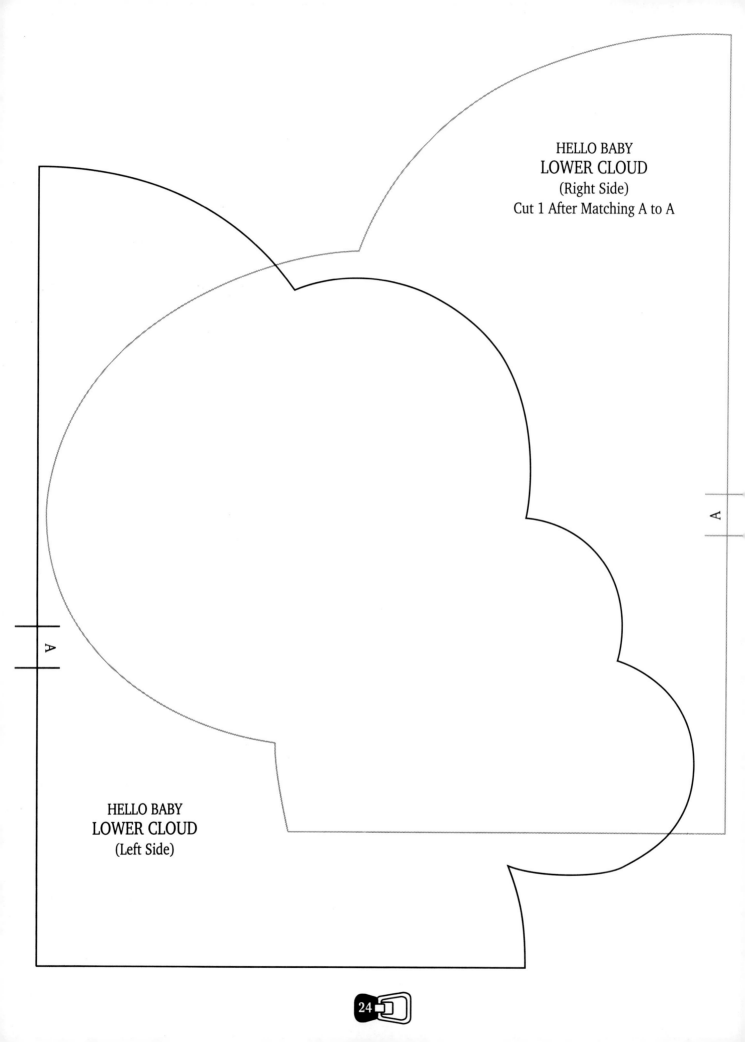

HELLO BABY
LOWER CLOUD
(Right Side)
Cut 1 After Matching A to A

A

A

HELLO BABY
LOWER CLOUD
(Left Side)

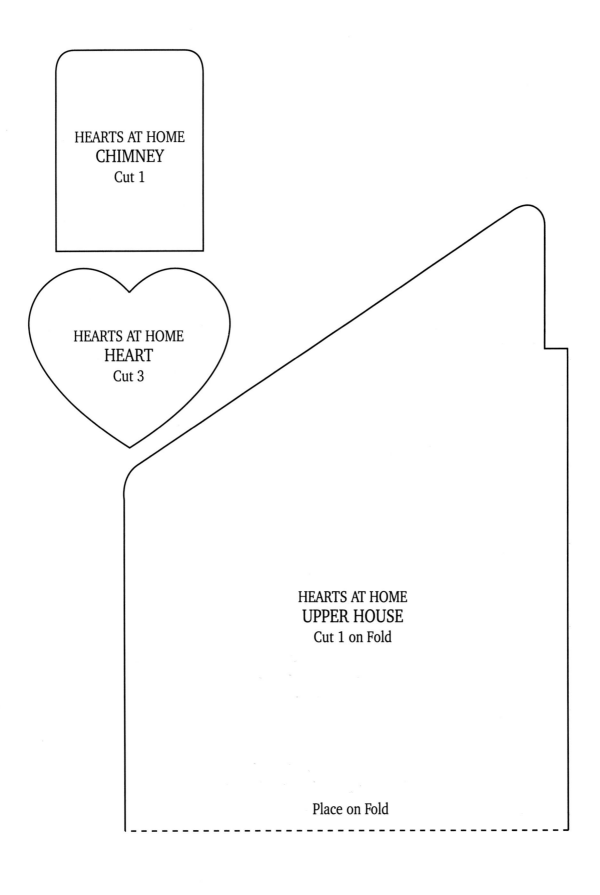

HEARTS AT HOME
CHIMNEY
Cut 1

HEARTS AT HOME
HEART
Cut 3

HEARTS AT HOME
UPPER HOUSE
Cut 1 on Fold

Place on Fold

EDUCATED PLACES
LOWER SCHOOL
Cut 1

HEARTS AT HOME
LOWER HOUSE
Cut 1

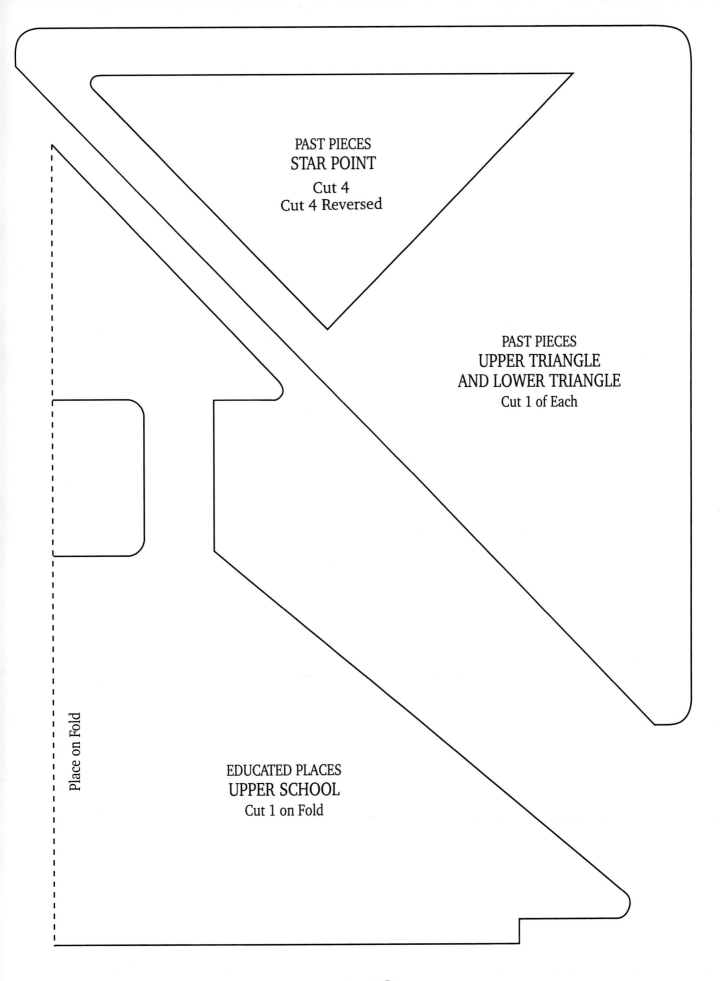

PAST PIECES
STAR POINT

Cut 4
Cut 4 Reversed

PAST PIECES
**UPPER TRIANGLE
AND LOWER TRIANGLE**

Cut 1 of Each

Place on Fold

EDUCATED PLACES
UPPER SCHOOL

Cut 1 on Fold

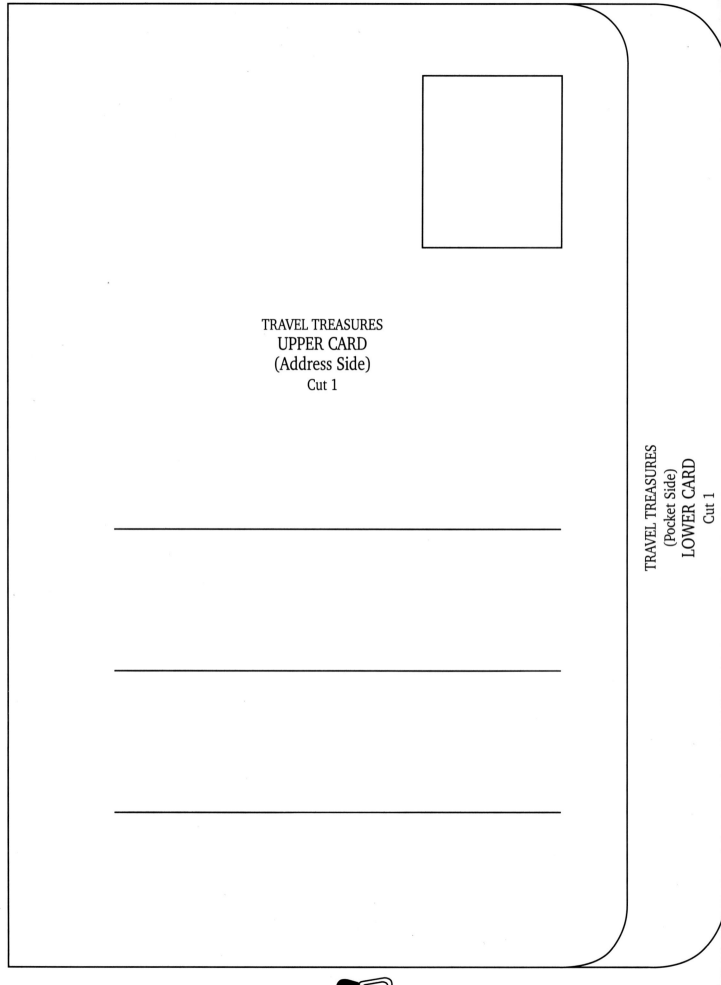

TRAVEL TREASURES
UPPER CARD
(Address Side)
Cut 1

TRAVEL TREASURES
(Pocket Side)
LOWER CARD
Cut 1